Gary
&
Lani,

Thank you so much
for partnering with us to
reach the world for christ!
we pray this christmas
is a wonderful & refreshing
time for you and your family!

In His Love,
Drew
&
Jen

Psalm 73:23-26

Moments Together

for

PARENTS

Dennis and Barbara Rainey

Regal

From Gospel Light
Ventura, California, U.S.A.

PUBLISHED BY REGAL BOOKS
FROM GOSPEL LIGHT
VENTURA, CALIFORNIA, U.S.A.
PRINTED IN THE U.S.A.

Regal Books is a ministry of Gospel Light, an evangelical Christian publisher dedicated to serving the local church. We believe God's vision for Gospel Light is to provide church leaders with biblical, user-friendly materials that will help them evangelize, disciple and minister to children, youth and families.

It is our prayer that this Regal book will help you discover biblical truth for your own life and help you meet the needs of others. May God richly bless you.

For a free catalog of resources from Regal Books/Gospel Light, please call your Christian supplier or contact us at 1-800-4-GOSPEL *or* www.regal books.com.

Rights for publishing this book in other languages are contracted by Gospel Light Worldwide, the international non-profit ministry of Gospel Light. Gospel Light Worldwide also provides publishing and technical assistance to international publishers dedicated to producing Sunday School and Vacation Bible School curricula and books in the languages of the world. For additional information, visit www.gospellightworldwide.org; write to Gospel Light World-wide, P.O. Box 3875, Ventura, CA 93006; or send an e-mail to info@gospellightworldwide.org.

Cover and interior design by Robert Williams
Edited by Bruce Nygren

Library of Congress Cataloging-in-Publication Data
Rainey, Dennis, 1948–
    Moments together for parents / Dennis and Barbara Rainey.
        p. cm.
Rev. ed. of: Moments together for couples. c1995.
    ISBN 0-8307-3249-7
    1.   Parents—Prayer-books and devotions—English.   I. Rainey, Barbara. II. Rainey, Dennis, 1948– Moments together for couples. III. Title.
    BV4845.R35 2003
    242′.645—dc21   2002156012

1   2   3   4   5   6   7   8   9   /   09   08   07   06   05   04   03

INTRODUCTION

Although some days it may not seem so, there's more to parenting than processing diapers, sopping up juice spills, settling sibling border wars, treating ear infections, listening to drum lessons, providing taxi service, supervising home-work, coaching soccer, shopping for prom dresses and apply-ing for second mortgages to fund a teen's car insurance!

How would you like a little time to sit down, slip off your shoes, speak several intelligible sentences to your spouse, discuss your parenting goals and pray? How about some time just for the two of you?

If such a break from the perils of parenting sounds good to you, this small book is destined to encourage you and have a huge impact on your life—and on your children's lives as well!

We know about the busyness and stress of leading a family in today's world. During our 29-year commitment to parenting, 6 Rainey protégés are either still growing their way through our home or already have flown to their own coops. We know how on some days you just hope you can survive until sundown—much less find time to prioritize your family's values or talk to God.

Moments Together for Parents is designed for the husband and wife that want to work as a team to obtain God's best blessings for their family tribe. These 30 brief devotionals not only create the window of opportunity to discuss God's instructions for the family and to pray, but they also give you both a reason to sit down and reconnect!

Here are some of the topics we cover:

- Creative ways to spend time with the kids
- Leading a child to Christ
- To spank or not to spank
- Confronting the TV monster
- Dates with sons and daughters
- Raising kids with a spiritual mission
- How to talk to a teenager
- The prayer of the helpless parent

Although we parents find some humor in the work and challenges involved in raising children, we certainly take very seriously the responsibility God has given us. We are not just attempting to raise good kids; we are preparing the next generation that will represent Christ on Earth and advance the gospel. Such a task demands that we spend some time making sure our plans are empowered by prayer and based upon the wisdom of God's blueprints for building a godly family.

Take a break from your parenting duties and approach God as a team through *Moments Together for Parents*. You will be so happy you did! And can't that load of clothes and that escaped hamster loose in the family room wait a few more minutes anyway?

God bless you as you participate in a family reformation—one home at a time!

Making the Most of It All

Therefore be careful how you walk, not as unwise men,
but as wise, making the most of your time.

EPHESIANS 5:15-16

Someday when the kids are gone, there will be plenty of ice cream just for Barbara and me. I won't find the can of Hershey's chocolate on the lower shelf—empty and with a sticky bottom. We will return to a small refrigerator and eat on the antique table we used when we were first married.

Cars will be clean again. The floorboard won't be covered with Sunday School papers or petrified McDonald's french fries. And gum, Legos, Matchbox cars, doll combs and even fishhooks won't be mushed into the carpet.

Doors will be shut, and I won't have to go through the house turning off every light. We won't stumble over herds of teddy bears, dolls and stuffed animals grazing or napping on the carpet.

Fewer tools will be lost. No frantic search parties at bedtime for lost blankets. Socks will miraculously find their mates, and the car keys will be right where I left them.

But of course other things will change, too.

When the kids are gone, we won't hear the pitter-patter of little feet running down the hallway and then feel a warm, wiggly body crawling into bed and snuggling with us early on Saturday morning.

No more frilly little-girl Easter dresses or first days of school. No winter picnics or log-cabin playhouses. No more fishing and hunting trips or wiener roasts or just goofing around with a childish hand in mine.

Someday there will be no more handmade Father's Day cards or wooden plaques titled "World's Best Mom." No more crayon drawings, verses and stick people drawn on construction paper and displayed on the refrigerator.

So until someday arrives, we're going to cherish our moments together. We're going to try to take seriously—but happily—the apostle Paul's counsel: "Mak[e] the most of your time." Sticky or not.

Discuss: What season of life are you in right now? Are you making the most of this time, fulfilling your responsibilities with contentment, joy and appreciation?

Pray: Ask for contentment and for the ability to focus on what God has called you to do presently.

RELATIONSHIPS REQUIRE TIME

*Therefore, my beloved brethren, be steadfast,
immovable, always abounding in the work of the Lord,
knowing that your toil is not in vain in the Lord.*

1 CORINTHIANS 15:58

What if you approached your mate after your wedding and said, "Now that we're married, please don't make me spend time with you"? Naturally your mate would say, "You're crazy! How can we build a marriage unless we spend time together?"

The same is true with your children. Barbara and I discovered that as our kids grew older and began to spend more and more time with friends, we had to work harder to spend time with them.

Be creative as you think of things you can do that your children would enjoy. Smaller children, for example, love things as simple as a trip to a convenience store to buy a candy bar or an ice-cream cone.

We have lived out in the country, so when we were in town with two cars, we needed to decide who would ride with

Mom and who would ride with Dad. Usually our two youngest girls said, "We want to go with Daddy." You know why? Because if I stopped for gas at the convenience store, they figured I was a soft touch; they would try to ease me on over to the ice-cream or candy section.

And you know what? I was—and am—a soft touch. I loved spending time with them. It was an opportunity to enjoy something together that they liked to do. Was it always fat free and super healthy? No, but it was healthy for the relationship.

A great thing to do with teenagers is to go shopping with them. My girls enjoyed shopping for clothes while the boys looked for sporting equipment. It wasn't the purchase that was important; it was the time we spent together.

Another great thing to do, which we're losing in today's culture, is reading to our kids. It is a real sacrifice of love and an easy way for both moms and dads to get involved with their kids. I once read *The Chronicles of Narnia* to one of my sons and he loved it!

I remember one night when my teenage son, Samuel, and I went to town to get some groceries and waste some time together without any agenda. His response? "Dad, I'm glad we just spent some time together without any big goals. It was great to be with you!"

When's the last time you wasted an evening with one of your children for no other reason than just being with them?

Discuss: Evaluate how you spend time with each of your children. Do you need to commit more time to your kids just doing things on their level?

Pray: Ask God to help you set more time aside just for your kids.

WE DISCOVERED
THAT AS OUR KIDS
GREW OLDER, WE HAD
TO WORK HARDER
TO SPEND TIME
WITH THEM.

At an Early Age

But Jesus said, "Let the children alone, and do not hinder them from coming to Me; for the kingdom of heaven belongs to such as these."

MATTHEW 19:14

How old does a child have to be before he or she can place saving faith in Jesus Christ? The great English preacher C. H. Spurgeon said, "A child who knowingly sins can savingly believe."

Many of the great leaders of the Church became Christians when they were very young. It was said of Polycarp, a first-century church leader, that he walked with God for 86 years before he died at the age of 95. Isaac Watts, the great hymn writer, came to saving faith in Christ at nine years of age.

I was six when I began to feel my need for forgiveness. I grew up in a church with a pastor who preached about heaven and hell, a couple of places we don't hear much about these days.

I recall becoming so aware of my sin that I would lie in bed and shudder; I was afraid to go to bed at night for fear that I'd die in my sleep and spend an eternity in hell.

So one Sunday I told my mom that I felt it was time for me to give my life to Christ. She talked straight to me about my decision, and she didn't hinder me from making my commitment public.

I recall walking down that church aisle with a lump in my throat; it was a public confession of wanting Jesus Christ to be my Savior and Lord. That decision marked my life. A few weeks later, my teacher asked me to draw a picture of what I wanted to do when I grew up. I will never forget that picture, because God had already etched His mark on my life. I drew a picture, of a stick-figure man preaching about Christ.

That was over 40 years ago. And thanks to my parents' faithful instruction, I can look back on that commitment as the most important decision in my life.

Discuss: Have your children made a decision to receive Christ? What can you do to help them understand the gospel?

Pray: Ask God to give you wisdom and clarity in teaching your children about God's forgiveness through faith in His Son, Jesus Christ.

A CHILD WHO
KNOWINGLY SINS
CAN SAVINGLY
BELIEVE.

DAY 4

A BURDEN OR A BLESSING?

Behold, children are a gift of the Lord; the fruit of
the womb is a reward. How blessed is the man
whose quiver is full of them.

PSALM 127:3,5

Many parents today feel like kids are a burden. That's not what the Bible calls them. It doesn't say, "Behold, children are a burden of the Lord," or "Burdened is the man whose quiver is full of them."

Our views have become distorted. What we see as a burden, God sees as a blessing. Some of us need to knock out the windows of our corrupted views and let the Spirit of God come into our homes and refresh our hearts and minds, so we can see clearly again that children are a blessing.

Don't get me wrong. Barbara and I will be the first to tell you we are still in process with our children. We have failed many times. And on occasion I have been so frustrated, after exhausting all rational reasoning, all reward systems and all biblical approaches, that the only thing left for me to do was yell, throw a box of tissues at the floor, slam the door and walk out—just like my kids did. This just convinces me that one of God's greatest purposes for parents is to bring us face-to-face with our own depravity.

We want life to be easy or at least bearable. And when children make our lives difficult, we begin to feel they are burdens. But we fail to realize what God makes clear—our children are gifts from God. God has given us our children for His glory and our good.

When I speak at our FamilyLife Marriage Conferences, I'm always struck by how surprised couples are when I explain that our mates are gifts from God. Why are they so astounded? Don't they know our God? He wants to bless us. He's out for our best interests!

In the same way, you need to receive your children as gifts from God. If you do, your whole attitude will change. No longer will you try to change your kids; no longer will you consider them burdens. Instead, you'll view them as true blessings from God entrusted to you.

Discuss: How do you view your children—as burdens or blessings?

Pray: With your mate, acknowledge your children as gifts from God.

GOD HAS GIVEN US
OUR CHILDREN
FOR HIS GLORY
AND OUR GOOD.

Managing a Monster

*Be on the alert, stand firm in the faith,
act like men, be strong.*

1 CORINTHIANS 16:13

Since much of what comes into our homes via television does not contribute to a sound Christian home, what can be done to manage this "monster"?

Why not start a Just Say No campaign against TV? I am not advocating total abstinence, although for some families that may be a good solution. But I do suggest taking TV in moderation—say, six to eight hours a week.

Here are some tips we have tried to follow in our family:

- Instruct the kids to ask you for permission to watch TV. Don't let them treat it as a given but a privilege. Don't let them watch it randomly, but determine what you want them to watch.
- Make TV off-limits in at least these two rooms: your bedroom and where you eat your meals.
- Agree on the number of hours and the programs that can be watched during the week and on week-ends. Let the kids choose from a list you approve.

- Don't let your children watch a video movie unless you know what's in it. Read the reviews of movies when they first appear at the theater to get clues about the level of bad language, sex and violence or get this kind of information from websites like www.christananswers.net/spotlight and www.screenit.com.
- Don't just watch TV: watch specific programs for a specific purpose. Once when I had plopped down to watch nothing in particular, Barbara said, "There's nothing on worth watching. There are other things more valuable to do, like spending time with me!" And she was right.

Yes, all this will take a great deal of self-control and discipline. But think of how the tube undermines the family, and you will realize it will be worth it. Statistics from TV-Free America show that half of four- to six-year-olds in the U.S. *would give up their relationships with their dads in favor of TV.*[1]

That's scary evidence of television's power. I believe God wants us to rule over this modern-day monster.

Discuss: Do you have rules about watching TV in your home? If not, talk about implementing some of the tips discussed above.

Pray: Ask that God's Spirit will enable each family member to identify and resist unhealthy influences.

Note

1. Norman Herr, "Television," *The Sourcebook for Teaching Science*, 2001. http://www.csun.edu/~vceed002/health/docs/tv&health.html (accessed December 3, 2002).

WHY NOT START A JUST SAY NO CAMPAIGN AGAINST TV?

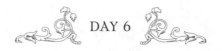

To Spank or Not to Spank?

*Foolishness is bound up in the heart
of a child; the rod of discipline will
remove it far from him.*

PROVERBS 22:15

What can make a child cry and a group of parents tense up like they are about to receive a shot at the doctor's office? It's the S word—"spanking."

Most of us know that the book of Proverbs affirms using "the rod of discipline" (Prov. 22:15). Because some parents have physically abused their children, an increasing number of people consider spanking to be synonymous with child abuse.

However, I believe properly administered spanking is a positive, biblical approach to raising children, provided you use two simple guidelines.

First, *clarify the boundaries and the punishments for the offenses.* Decide which behaviors are worth a spanking, and be sure your child understands it. We have six children and only have enforced half a dozen issues warranting a spanking.

Spanking has been used sparingly and as a last resort in the training of our children. But we have used it.

Second, *spanking should not be administered in anger but in love and in the context of a relationship with the child.* The purpose is to help the child understand that his or her wrong choices have consequences. We always loved on our children before and after they'd been disciplined. I didn't get that many spankings as a child, but I can tell you this: I always felt loved, and I definitely needed the correction!

As parents, we are in the process of producing a harvest of character, helping our children learn to be responsive to God and themselves for their lives. As parents, we can't gloss over flagrant disobedience and pretend it didn't occur. If we do, we allow foolishness, rather than wisdom, to have a foothold in our children's hearts.

Discuss: Are you and your spouse in agreement when it comes to disciplining your child? What are your boundaries and the penalties for crossing them?

Pray: Ask God to give you the courage to follow the Scriptures in your family. Ask Him to help you achieve that blend of authority and love that tells your children that you really care about them.

As parents, we are
in the process of
producing a harvest
of character
in our children.

THE CASE FOR TENDER MEN

Be kind to one another, tender-hearted.

EPHESIANS 4:32

I wonder how many men read Ephesians 4:32 and think, *That doesn't apply to me.* From an early age, many men are taught not to cry, not to show feelings, not to be tender toward their wife and children.

There is a real need in our nation right now for men to be fathers who love and lead their families—who are not afraid to be tender.

I heard of a young woman whose story illustrates this point. Desperate to reach out to her unfeeling father, she got herself arrested for shoplifting. That didn't work, so she decided to stop eating. She developed anorexia and, later, a brain tumor that the doctors said was caused in part by her undernourished condition.

"I was lying in my hospital bed near death with all kinds of tubes coming out of my body when my father finally came to see me," the woman recalled. "We talked for about an hour; then he got up to leave. As he opened my hospital door, I guess I just went berserk. I began to scream, 'You just can't say it, can you?'" She screamed even louder, "I'm going to die and you still can't say it!"

Her father said, "Say what?"

"I love you," she said.

He finally broke down and began to weep. He moved to her bedside and through his tears said those words the young woman needed to hear so desperately.

Fathers need to be tender. Their hearts need to be knitted to their children's souls. Real men can be gentle men.

Discuss: When was the last time you told your children you loved them? Your wife? Ask your spouse what tender love for a child looks like from his or her perspective.

Pray: Ask God to develop your heart so that you will be able to communicate the tender side of love to your wife and children.

FATHERS NEED TO
BE TENDER. THEIR HEARTS
NEED TO BE
KNITTED TO THEIR
CHILDREN'S SOULS.

PLUGGING IN TO GOD

Be strong and courageous, do not be afraid or tremble at them, for the Lord your God is the one who goes with you. He will not fail you or forsake you.

DEUTERONOMY 31:6

Families should be a place of security and a place where parents teach their children that ultimate security is in God's hands, not theirs.

One morning as I pulled out of our garage to go to the airport, my daughter Ashley, then a preteen, rushed out to give me one more hug. I could tell something was troubling her. Reaching out through the car window to hold her hand, I asked, "What's wrong, princess?"

"I'm afraid your airplane is going to crash," she said, obviously a bit embarrassed by her admission. A recent airplane crash in Dallas had sent unsettling shock waves of fear through my daughter.

"Planes are safer than driving, Ashley," I said reassuringly. "Besides, my life is in God's hands and He knows what He's doing." By now my tenderhearted young Ashley was clutching my hand in both of hers, and I could see that my theological lesson had fallen short of its mark. Fear was visible on her face.

I went on to explain that fear is a normal emotion but that she could give it to God. "You're in the process of learning how to depend less on me and more on Him," I said. "I won't always be here to answer your questions—but God will. Now it's as if there are invisible electrical cords coming from you to me and your mom. And our responsibility is to unplug those cords from us and teach you how to plug them in to God."

I then took one of her hands and gently unplugged one of those invisible strands from me. She frowned and then grinned as I guided her hand above her head and helped her visualize plugging in to God. "Ashley," I said as I tenderly squeezed her hand, "I need to go, and you're going to have to take your fear to Jesus Christ. He can give you the peace."

As I pulled out of the driveway, I waved at Ashley and she grinned back. I thought about how the culture she was growing up in did not know where to plug in. I was glad I could point her to the Lord.

Discuss: Are there any areas of your life that aren't plugged in? What can you do to begin teaching your children how to become dependent upon God?

Pray: Ask God to enable you to model a life that is plugged in to God.

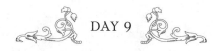

GOD'S MOMENTS FOR MOM

BY BARBARA RAINEY

And let us not lose heart in doing good, for in due time we shall reap if we do not grow weary.

GALATIANS 6:9

For me, being a mom is both my greatest joy and my area of greatest challenge and worry. But sometimes I believe God gives mothers special fulfilling moments to keep us hanging in there.

One day my daughter Ashley and I went shopping, and as we came in carrying all the bags, a big bottle of cream rinse fell out of Ashley's arms, hit the garage floor and splattered everywhere. All I could say was, "Oh, Ashley!" Though I didn't form the words, my voice implied, "How could you be so careless?"

After cleaning up the mess, I went inside and suggested that the kids help pick up the house a bit. Ashley made an uncharacteristic comment about the house being so messy it wouldn't make much difference anyway. My pride was offended at the truth of her statement, but I said nothing.

That night I found a note from Ashley: "Dear Mommy, I am sorry I called your house a messy place. Will you forgive me? And the rinse breaking. It was dumb. I hope you and I can go shopping again. Love you more than you can imagine. Love in Christ. Ashley."

One Christmas I received a similar note that also took me from the depths to the heights. I had bawled out Benjamin for messing up his bedroom. Afterward I said, "Benjamin, all you are going to remember about me is that I griped at you and I yelled about picking up your room."

That night he gave me a note: "Thank you for being a great mom. That's what I will remember the most. I love you, Benjamin."

Yes, being a mother can be challenging, hard, frustrating and lonely; but there are those priceless moments that come every day in the form of a note, a quick hug and a kiss, or something said as only a child can say it.

Discuss: What part of being a parent do you find the most rewarding? Frustrating? Recall a time when one of your children made being a parent all worthwhile.

Pray: Ask God to empower you with wisdom, equip you with patience and reward you with joy in the challenge of parenting.

KIDS AND THE IMAGE OF GOD

*And God created man in His own image,
in the image of God He created him; male
and female He created them.*

GENESIS 1:27

How do you communicate to your children that they are cherished and accepted both by you and by God, while still holding up realistic standards for them?

The world places a premium upon performance. As a result, three false values have arisen: intellect, beauty and athletic ability. You must respect your children's uniquenesses above the imposing pressures of the world's value system, showing that they are made in God's image regardless of performance.

It's also difficult to build self-esteem when parents have differing expectations. Consider the boy who grows up with a father who wants him to be aggressive, competitive and outgoing. Add a mother who desires a quiet, calm "mommy's boy." The result is a son caught in a vice, unable to please either of his parents.

Your own upbringing influences your ability to communicate reasonable expectations. If your parents held unachievable standards over you, you will tend to do the same thing to your children, even though you fight fiercely to avoid it.

What can you do to correct unreal expectations? First, *know your child*. Know his or her true abilities and interests. Each child should be uniquely considered, apart from siblings.

Second, *clearly verbalize your expectations*. Unfortunately, many standards are never spoken until they are violated. One suggestion: Write down all the major expectations you hold for your child and post them on a personalized bulletin board.

Third, *praise your children for genuine effort*. Warm praise and respect will encourage the growth of positive self-esteem. You might ask yourself, *How many times do I positively reinforce my child for his or her efforts each day?* Don't be guilty of withholding your approval from your children. Lavishly grant approval of a job well done.

Discuss: On a scale of 1 to 10, with 1 at the top, rank your parents' expectations of you as a child. Discuss with your mate how those expectations affect you and your parenting style today.

Pray: Ask that you can experience God's acceptance in order to communicate acceptance and self-esteem to your children.

YOU MUST RESPECT
YOUR CHILDREN'S
UNIQUENESSES ABOVE
THE IMPOSING
PRESSURES OF THE
WORLD'S VALUE SYSTEM.

LEAVE SOME FOR HOME

*An overseer . . . must be one who manages
his own household well, keeping his children
under control with all dignity.*

1 TIMOTHY 3:2-4

$\mathcal{T}$he apostle Paul required that an overseer in the Early Church be a man who was a good manager of his household. My dad was that kind of man. I remember him as a man of quiet authority, who had time for us.

What kind of memories will your children have of you as a father? Will they remember a father who spent time with them, played with them, laughed with them? Or will they think of you as someone who was preoccupied with work, unfinished projects or a hobby?

And now let's really get personal: What would happen if you switched the energy you give to your job with the energy you give to your home and family? What would happen to work? What would happen to your home?

I realize this may be an unfair question because by necessity many men work long hours away from home. But too many fathers give almost all of their energy to their jobs and leave none for their families.

I have a friend who has a 3x5-inch card on his desk that reads "Leave some for home."

He realizes that without this reminder shouting at him daily, he'd go home with no energy most of the time. His job is that draining.

We need to balance things out if the next generation is to get the kind of leadership it needs. Today we need fathers who are determined to save the energy to succeed at home, regardless of the cost.

As leaders and managers of our homes, we can't lead from afar. We've got to be there. And be all there!

Discuss: As a father, what areas of home life do you find the most challenging to manage? How about time management? Do you make time to be present and available for each member of your family?

Pray: Ask God to give you, as a father, the spirit of a servant and the strength of an overseer who manages his household well.

WHAT WOULD HAPPEN
IF YOU SWITCHED THE ENERGY
YOU GIVE TO YOUR JOB WITH
THE ENERGY YOU GIVE TO
YOUR HOME AND FAMILY?

THE PRAYER OF THE HELPLESS PARENT

"Not by might nor by power, but by My Spirit,"
says the Lord of hosts.

ZECHARIAH 4:6

No one raises perfect kids. No one is the perfect parent. No one does it all.

Barbara and I have discovered a secret, though, and it's the greatest one of all: *God helps parents raise their kids.* He delights when we admit our weaknesses because that's when He gives us wisdom and power through the Holy Spirit. He loves the prayer of the helpless parent.

I think that God uses our kids to get our attentions. He wants to rule in our lives, but as long as we feel we can succeed in our own power, we won't listen to His Spirit.

Psalm 127:1 says, "Unless the Lord builds the house, they labor in vain who build it." God will help you build your house. You can do it with Him as the architect and builder.

There's a gravel road in the country where I go jogging, and I like to pray for my family as I run. Often I cry out to the Lord, "Unless You build this house, it isn't going to work. You know the parents here. You know the children. Lord, You gave them to us, so help us be successful in raising them."

Pray to God for help in building your home. Pray that you might keep your marriage holy and pure. Ask Him to give you wisdom, strong and resilient commitments, pure romance and vital relationships.

Ask God to help you, the helpless parent. Ask Him to get your child's attention. Plead with Him to build convictions where you can't. Ask Him to build your home. God loves the prayer of the helpless parent.

Discuss: What makes you feel helpless as a parent? What's happening in your family right now that pushes you to depend on God?

Pray: Spend some time in prayer, asking God to give you specific wisdom and guidance for the decisions you face as a parent right now.

ASK GOD TO
HELP YOU, THE
HELPLESS
PARENT.

LAUNCHING OUR ARROWS

Like arrows in the hand of a warrior, so are the children of one's youth.

PSALM 127:4

I find it interesting that the Scripture describes children as "arrows" because arrows are meant to be released. As we have raised our children, Barbara and I knew we were responsible to prepare them to live independently.

All of our efforts as parents were made with the knowledge that, eventually, these arrows would be flying on their own. We made a conscious effort to give them skills in living and in making godly choices.

There's an important characteristic of an arrow: It is an offensive weapon. God wants every Christian to make an impact in the world for Christ, and He wants us parents to emphasize this vision as we raise our children.

When I drove our kids to school, I prayed for them: "Lord, I pray that they will never forget that they are Your representatives at school today. I pray that they will be lights in the midst of the darkness."

Knowing we will release our kids, however, doesn't make it any easier when the time actually comes. The twang of our bowstring was first heard in August of 1993 when we took our oldest child, Ashley, to college. I remember the scene well: Barbara, Ashley and I stood in the dorm parking lot, huddled up, arms entwined, sobbing. I was crying so hard that I couldn't pray; my own daughter had to pray for herself!

As we drove away from the dorm, my "little girl" stood on the sidewalk, waving good-bye. I turned to Barbara and said, "One down and five to go! Can you believe that in a year we've got to do this again with Benjamin?"

I paused for a moment. The tears were drying on my face, but the pain of the loss was fresh. "This hurts too much," I said. "I'm not doing it next year. I'm going to rent a dad for a day to do it for me!"

Discuss: Are you preparing to launch your arrows as offensive weapons? What can you begin doing now to give your children a mind-set of helping reach people for Christ?

Pray: Thank God for the privilege of having influence on the direction your arrows fly. Ask Him to always keep His target in front of you.

THE GREENHOUSE

For He established a testimony in Jacob.

PSALM 78:5

We all know the last words of Christ before He ascended to heaven—the Great Commission of Matthew 28:18-20, where He commands us to "make disciples of all the nations."

I'd like to point you to another passage in which God lays out an important part of His plan to fulfill that commission. Psalm 78:5-7 reads:

> For He established a testimony in Jacob, and appointed a law in Israel, which He commanded our fathers, that they should teach them to their children, that the generation to come might know, even the children yet to be born, that they may arise and tell them to their children, that they should put their confidence in God, and not forget the works of God, but keep His commandments.

As I read Scripture, I see that God formed two institutions to pass His Word from one generation to the next. One, of course, is His Church. The other is the *family*. God's original plan called for the home to be a sort of greenhouse—a nurture center—where children grow up to learn godly character and biblical values.

As a parent, it's so easy to get caught up in the pressures of daily living: changing diapers, settling sibling disputes and ferrying kids to piano lessons and scout meetings. From time to time you must look above that and remember that the most important work during your years on Earth will be to teach your children how to know and love the Lord God. Through your words and your actions—*your very life*—you have the power to shape the future of our nation by shaping a few of the people who live in it.

I love what Charles Swindoll says about the importance of a family and a home in this process:

> Whatever else may be said about the home, it is the bottom line of life. The anvil upon which attitudes and convictions are hammered out. It's the place where life's bills come due, the single most influential force in our earthly existence. . . . It is at home, among family members, that we come to terms with circumstances. It is here life makes up its mind.[1]

Discuss: What convictions and values do you want to pass on to your children?

Pray: Ask God to give you wisdom in raising the next generation and imparting to them biblical values.

Note

1. Charles Swindoll, *Home Is Where Life Makes Up Its Mind* (Portland, OR: Multnomah Press, 1979), p. 5.

THE MOST IMPORTANT
WORK DURING YOUR
YEARS ON EARTH WILL BE
TO TEACH YOUR CHILDREN
HOW TO KNOW AND
LOVE THE LORD GOD.

WHAT CHILDREN NEED TO KNOW

For all have sinned and fall short of the glory of God,
being justified as a gift by His grace through the
redemption which is in Christ Jesus.

ROMANS 3:23-24

I believe many parents today think their children are too young to understand the gospel, yet many children understand faith at an early age—our own six children all indicated they received Christ before the age of six.

Many don't realize God has given them one of the finest tools for teaching spiritual truth—the family. Kids can learn about biblical truth through their relationships with their parents and their siblings.

Even the deepest truths of a book such as Romans can be brought to life to a child. For example, kids learn of their mistakes within a family. They see their own tendency to be selfish, to disobey and to sin within a family. You can explain a verse such as Romans 3:23 to them by using their selfishness as an example of what it means to "fall short of the glory of God."

Or take the concept of forgiveness. From a very early age, Barbara and I taught our children that when they disobey a parent or hurt a brother or sister, they need to go and ask that person for forgiveness. They learned the process of forgiveness within the family, and we referred to those experiences when we explained the gospel to them. We hurt God with our sins, and we need to come to Him and ask for forgiveness.

I am not trivializing God's forgiveness. We just need to think as a child thinks and go back to the very basic elements of the faith. Once children understand their need for forgiveness, we then explain the basis for God's forgiveness—the sacrifice of His Son, Jesus Christ.

The family is a divine incubator for teaching spiritual truths. We need to use it when teaching the fundamentals of faith to our kids.

Discuss: Children need to understand the basics of the gospel message in order to come to Christ. First, they need to be taught who God is and how He loves them. Second, children must realize that their sins need to be forgiven. Finally, children need to understand that God's forgiveness comes through Jesus Christ. Think of how you could illustrate these concepts to them through experiences within your family.

Pray: As a couple, ask that God's Spirit would speak through you to touch your children's hearts with their need for Christ.

THE FAMILY IS A
DIVINE INCUBATOR
FOR TEACHING
SPIRITUAL TRUTHS.

AN ENCOURAGING WORD

*And let us consider how to stimulate one
another to love and good deeds.*

HEBREWS 10:24

I once was speaking to a group of several hundred singles, and I asked, "How many of you grew up in homes where you were told you were great?" Perhaps a dozen raised their hands. The rest of these young adults remembered words of criticism from their parents more than they remembered words of encouragement.

When was the last time you pondered how to encourage those in your family? If you want your mate to live a godly life, if you would like to see your children grow up to love the Lord and walk with Him, then you need to make encouragement a part of your daily vocabulary.

I remember watching a PBS special in which Daniel Boorstein, then the head Librarian of Congress, brought out a little blue box that contained the contents of Abraham Lincoln's pockets on the night he was assassinated. Among the contents were several news clippings applauding

Lincoln's leadership and great deeds. It's easy to forget that when Lincoln lived, millions of people hated him, and he needed encouragement like anyone else.

All of us have an encouragement meter that is near empty at times. In fact, has anybody ever been encouraged too much? Have you ever felt too appreciated?

I've got a challenge for you. Spend some time thinking of five good things about each member of your family. Begin writing them here, and use additional paper as needed.

1.	1.
2.	2.
3.	3.
4.	4.
5.	5.

Now commit yourself to finding time to encourage each family member in these areas during the next week. Spend more time encouraging than criticizing.

Be warned though: Do not wait for somebody to praise you. Someone once said, "You can sometimes catch a terrible chill waiting for someone else to cover you with glory."

Discuss: Share your lists for each child.

Pray: Ask that God would cement good qualities in each family member through your encouragement.

If you would like to see your children grow up to love the Lord and walk with Him, then you need to make encouragement a part of your daily vocabulary.

The Risk of Responsibility

*And we urge you, brethren, admonish the unruly, encourage
the fainthearted, help the weak, be patient with all men.*

1 THESSALONIANS 5:14

In his best-seller *The Third Wave*, Alvin Toffler wrote that
much teenage rebellion occurs because teenagers no longer
feel needed by the family unit nor economically productive
during the prolonged adolescent years.[1] Children need to be
given jobs to do in the home, partly because of their need to
be needed.

This can be difficult for perfectionistic parents. But, for
example, if you want to train your children to clean the
kitchen, you've got to lower your expectations of what a
clean kitchen looks like—at least initially. If you want to
teach your child to help with the laundry, you've got to
expect clumsy folding jobs. And if you dare to help your
child learn how to cook, be ready to put up with spills, splat-
ters and splashes.

None of our children was a neat freak. Ashley, our oldest,
was a pack rat. She wanted a souvenir from every exciting

moment of her life. Benjamin was the champion of expediency. He wanted to put off his cleaning chores because "If I vacuum now, it'll be dirty again by tonight." (Unfortunately, he was right.) Deborah was our resident artist. She started picking up the playroom, but before long she was decorating the room—or herself.

Yet we wanted our children to come to maturity. If we expected them to learn dependability, we had to depend on them. If we wanted our children to learn responsibility, we had to risk this gap between our expectations and their performances.

Discuss: How does your family divide household chores? Do any of your children complain that their part is unfair? What jobs do you sometimes think you should do yourself rather than risk children doing them inadequately?

Pray: Ask for the courage to risk allowing your children to be children, as well as for their continued growth toward maturity and increasing dependability.

Note
1. Alvin Toffler, *The Third Wave* (New York: Morrow, 1980), n.p.

CHILDREN NEED TO
BE NEEDED.

A DATE WITH ASHLEY

But we proved to be gentle among you, as a nursing mother tenderly cares for her own children.

1 THESSALONIANS 2:7

Unlike some stereotypes of macho men, it's important for dads to be as gentle as Paul was with the Thessalonians, his children in the faith.

I'll never forget the rewards I've received for trying to be tender and loving with my children. My first "date" with our daughter Ashley was when she was three. I called her from the office and said, "Hi, this is Dad. I would really like to have a special date with you tonight, Princess."

She giggled and I heard her tiny voice saying, "Daddy wants to take me out on a *date!*" Barbara already knew my plan, so Ashley was all dressed up by the time I pulled up in front of the house. I knocked on the door and when Barbara opened it, I said, "Hello, ma'am. Is your daughter home?"

Ashley came out, and we held hands as we walked down the steps of the front porch out to the car. I walked around to her door and opened it and she got in.

As we drove down the road, she slipped her little arm around my neck. We went to a restaurant and got chocolate pie, chocolate milk and chocolate ice cream. Then we went to a movie. Ashley had a great time crawling all over the seats and occasionally watching *Bambi*. We ate popcorn. We spilled popcorn. We got soft drinks, and we spilled soft drinks. We did it all, and we did it right.

After the movie we drove home, the faint green light from the Rambler dashboard shining in our faces. I turned and asked, "Ashley, what was your favorite thing about tonight?"

Her little hand came over to pat me on the arm and she said, "Just being with you, Dad, just being with you." It's too bad we didn't have a little more popcorn. I became a pool of melted butter right there.

Discuss: As a man, do you find it hard to be tender and intimate with your children? Describe some times when your attempts to be tender with them really worked.

Pray: As a father, pray that your need to be a strong leader will not conflict with being gentle and tender with every member of your family.

RAISING KIDS WITH A SENSE OF MISSION

Go therefore and make disciples of all the nations, baptizing them in the name of the Father and the Son and the Holy Spirit, teaching them to observe all that I commanded you; and lo, I am with you always, even to the end of the age.

MATTHEW 28:19-20

One day my pastor, Bill Parkinson, exhorted me with a thought-provoking question: "What if you reach the end of your life and the Great Commission is accomplished, and you had no part in it?"

Christ commands us to "make disciples of all the nations." Do you realize that your most important disciples are your own children? I especially wish more mothers had this vision. The enemy is trying to get moms to devalue their positions, so they won't raise the next generation to go to the world and have an impact for Christ.

If you want to raise your children with a sense of mission, begin when they are young by talking to them of God's plan. Then help them reach out to their peers.

Is one of your children a strong-willed child? She is the kind who will storm a country for Christ. He will be the one who never quits until he impacts his sphere of influence.

Pray for their mates with them. Why do I put mate in with mission? Because the mate will determine a great deal of what is accomplished in that mission.

Next, teach them they are pilgrims in this world, not wanderers. A wanderer is aimless. A pilgrim must travel lightly if he is to get where he needs to go. I believe a sense of mission will emerge if you shape their convictions.

Finally, give them the freedom to allow God to work in their lives. Affirm their decisions and direction as they get older. Do you know what the biggest deterrent is to missions today? It's parents who want their kids to make money and be successful!

When Jesus Christ washed the disciples' feet and went to the cross, He gave them the torch of the Great Commission that has been passed down throughout all of history. Our responsibility is to lead our own children to Christ and to give them a sense of mission to reach the next generation.

Discuss: How are you helping build the Great Commission right where you are?

Pray: Ask God to send laborers into the harvest. "The harvest is plentiful, but the workers are few" (Matt. 9:37).

DO YOU REALIZE
THAT YOUR MOST
IMPORTANT DISCIPLES
ARE YOUR OWN
CHILDREN?

WRONG WAY RIEGELS

I can do all things through Him who strengthens me.

PHILIPPIANS 4:13

*I*t is surprising to learn how many parents feel inadequate and helpless. I can relate to this because Barbara and I struggled as much as anyone else with these feelings. We knew we were not raising little robots that dutifully went about perfectly obeying us. We moaned over our failures and wondered if our kids would ever turn out right.

Have you heard of Wrong Way Riegels? Roy Riegels played in the 1929 Rose Bowl for the University of California and made one of the most famous mistakes in the history of football. He picked up a fumble, looked up and saw nothing but green grass ahead of him. He ran more than 60 yards—in the wrong direction! Finally he was tackled by his teammate inside their own 10-yard line. California was forced to punt, and Georgia Tech blocked the kick and scored.

At halftime, the California coach gave a rousing call to his dispirited team. At the end he declared, "Same team that started the first half, will start the second half." This meant that Roy was going to start the second half.

All the players ran out to the field except Roy. "Coach, I cannot go out there," Roy said. "I'm humiliated."

The coach looked Roy in the face and said, "Roy, the game is only half over. Now get out there and play the rest of it."[1]

The words of that coach are worth remembering today if you're a parent. You may have a 9-year-old, and you're thinking, *The game is half over—in 9 years he will be going to college*. Or your oldest may be 12 or 15 or 25. You look back with regret at your mistakes in parenting, and you think you've already lost the game.

It is at this point where we need the encouragement of Charles Spurgeon, who said, "It was by perseverance that the snail reached the ark."[2]

You cannot change what happened in the past; neither can I. What you can change is what you do in the future.

Discuss: Do you feel like a failure as a parent? Why?

Pray: Ask God to encourage you not to grow weary in doing good as a parent. Ask Him to show you how you can encourage your spouse in the battle.

Notes

1. James S. Hewett, ed., *Illustrations Unlimited* (Wheaton, IL: Tyndale House, 1990), n.p.
2. Mark Water, comp., *The New Encyclopedia of Christian Quotations* (Grand Rapids, MI: Baker Books, 2000), p. 728.

HELPING YOUR CHILDREN MAINTAIN INNOCENCE

*So that He may establish your hearts unblamable
in holiness before our God and Father.*

1 THESSALONIANS 3:13

How can you help your children stay pure sexually? I have a few suggestions.

First, *remember that your relationship with your child is the bridge into his or her life.* In war, the enemy wants to isolate you and cut off your supply line. Today the enemy wants to cut you off from your teenagers; then he can isolate them and convince them of anything.

Second, *give your preteens and teens some limits that will challenge them.* Barbara and I challenged our children not to kiss a member of the opposite sex until the wedding kiss. You may think this sounds puritanical (compared to the world, it is), but we believed that such a high standard would help them control their sexual urges.

In addition, we helped them set standards that would aid them in responding to many of the temptations our culture offers. We could not insulate them from the world, but we could encourage them to avoid viewing television shows and movies that have sexual content.

Finally, *ask your teenager to become accountable to you.* Accountability means staying involved in your teenager's life by asking some tough questions.

After church one time, my son went over to a young lady's home. I asked, "Her mom's there, right? What time will you be home?" I came by this training naturally because my mom used to bug me to death about where I had been, where I was going and when I would be home.

As you hold standards up for your teenager, be sure to explain some of the reasons God commanded us to abstain from sexual immorality: freedom from guilt and emotional scars, freedom from sexually transmitted diseases and unwanted pregnancies, and preservation of a gift that can only be given to one person—the gift of innocence. He has our best in mind.

And, please, after you've decided what boundaries you will draw for your children, remind them that if they fail, there is grace and forgiveness—from God and from you.

Discuss: Talk with your mate about the worst thing that could happen if you challenge your children not to kiss until they are married. Now discuss the worst consequence of not having a standard.

Pray: Ask God to help you get your boundaries and standards from the Scriptures and not the world.

DAY 22

PROTECTING YOUR CHILDREN'S INNOCENCE

For I am jealous for you with a godly jealousy;
for I betrothed you to one husband, that to Christ
I might present you as a pure virgin.

2 CORINTHIANS 11:2

When our oldest daughter, Ashley, was 16, she was allowed to date. But I made it clear I wanted to interview any boys who asked her out.

I still remember that first interview. Kevin showed up at my office riding his motorcycle (?!). I bought him a soft drink to keep things as informal as possible, and after several minutes of small talk, I looked him in the eye.

"You know, Kevin, I was a teenage boy once," I said. "And I want you to know that I remember what the sex drive is like for an 18-year-old young man." His eyes were getting bigger—he was really listening.

"I expect you to treat my daughter just like God would have you treat His finest creation—with all respect and dignity. Whether you go out with her 1 time or 100 times, I want to be able to look you in the eyes and ask you if you are treating my daughter with respect and dignity—especially in the physical area. God may want her to be another man's wife, so you better be very careful to keep this relationship pure."

On my way home I wondered if I was being too intrusive. Then over dinner my doubts evaporated when I shared what had happened.

It wasn't just Ashley who responded with appreciation. It was Benjamin, who was 14 at the time, who put it all in context. He said, "You know, Dad, I hope that the father of a girl I ask out wants to meet with me. I'll know I'm at the right house if that happens!"

The reason I met with Kevin is that I believed Barbara and I, as parents, were entrusted by God to protect our children's innocence. I'm convinced that parents need to possess a godly jealousy that ruthlessly protects our children from evil.

Discuss: Have you thought of how you want to protect your children in the sexual area when they become teenagers? What guidelines will you set?

Pray: Ask that God will give you a godly jealousy for your children and that your children will value and respect your role as protector and nourisher.

I'M CONVINCED THAT
PARENTS NEED TO
POSSESS A GODLY
JEALOUSY THAT RUTHLESSLY
PROTECTS OUR
CHILDREN FROM EVIL.

TALKING WITH TEENAGERS

(PART ONE)

That they may arise and tell them to their children,
that they should put their confidence in God, and not forget
the works of God, but keep His commandments.

PSALM 78:6-7

One day my son Benjamin was standing in the kitchen, nibbling on some barbecue potato chips. We hadn't really had any substantive, meaningful conversations in a week or more, so I'm certain I stunned him with a question I asked for no other reason than to stay connected with a 14-year-old boy going through puberty. I asked, "You been keeping your mind clean at school, son?"

I paused for emphasis, not that the question needed any help. Then I added, "You know, pornography—the kind of sleazy stuff boys pass around and look at?"

He looked me straight in the eye with a half-grin, like I'd been reading his mail, and said, "Funny you should ask. Today at school a friend brought a *Penthouse* magazine into the locker room. But I didn't look at it. I just turned and walked out."

"Good for you! Good for you!" I said twice, to let my affirming words soak into this growing boy's heart. The big grin that made its way across his face told me he was proud he had done what was right.

The sad truth is that many parents just don't have the nerve to ask teenagers such an intrusive question. It's as if something happens to parents when their kids become teenagers and they don't know how to talk to them.

Adolescence is the age when kids should be learning how to bring their Christian faith into the realities of every-day life. It's one thing to teach your kids about God, as Psalm 78 says to do, but it's quite another thing to teach them how to walk with God and avoid temptations such as pornography.

I'll let you in on another secret: Your teenagers probably want you to talk to them. And if you doubt that, I've got some proof in the next devotional.

Discuss: Why is it so threatening to talk to teenagers about such critical issues as pornography? As a couple, discuss your level of comfort.

Pray: Pray for one another that your faith would be marked by the same courage that the Old Testament saints used to battle their enemies.

ADOLESCENCE IS THE
AGE WHEN KIDS SHOULD
BE LEARNING HOW TO
BRING THEIR CHRISTIAN
FAITH INTO THE REALITIES
OF EVERYDAY LIFE.

TALKING WITH TEENAGERS
(PART TWO)

These commandments that I give you today are to be upon your hearts. Impress them on your children. Talk about them when you sit at home and when you walk along the road, when you lie down and when you get up.

DEUTERONOMY 6:6-7 (NIV)

Yes, I know all about teenagers—their bravado, their "I know it all" attitude. I know they often think their parents are stupid. But regardless of how they act, they still desire to have meaningful conversations with you.

If you doubt that, here's some evidence. A few years ago my church's youth pastors gave the youth group a two-question survey. Here's a sampling of their answers to question one: What subject do you wish you could have someone else ask your parents to discuss with you?

- Petting
- Marriage
- Sex

- Grades
- Allowance
- Dating
- Marijuana
- Drugs
- Using the car
- Curfew
- God
- Drinking
- Guys
- Friends
- Making my own decisions
- Their divorce
- Dating relationships
- Big responsibilities
- Bathing suits
- Peer pressure
- Love
- Beliefs of my own
- Me
- My faults
- Boyfriend problems
- Girls
- Money
- College
- Overcoming failures in my Christian walk

And you're wondering what you can talk to your teenagers about? What an opportunity to help them learn how to make choices that honor God in the problems they face on a daily basis.

Discuss: If you have a teenager, give him or her an assignment to answer this question: What are some things that you would like to talk about with us? Have your teenager circle his or her top three choices on the list on the previous page.

Pray: Ask God for His favor upon you, as parents, as you raise teens during these dangerous days.

I'LL LET YOU IN ON
A SECRET:
YOUR TEENAGERS
PROBABLY WANT YOU
TO TALK TO THEM.

TALKING WITH TEENAGERS

(PART THREE)

Nathan then said to David, "You are the man!"

2 SAMUEL 12:7

King David was on the hot seat. He had slept with Bathsheba and then sent her husband off to be killed at war. When the prophet Nathan approached him with a hypothetical case of a man who committed the same sin, David responded by saying the man deserved to die. Imagine his shock when Nathan cried, "You are the man!"

I think of that verse because parents should be prepared to be on the hot seat when they talk with teenagers. If you are not living the life you are telling them to live, they will let you know it.

In the same survey mentioned in the previous devotional, the youth at our church were asked, "What questions would you like to ask your parents if someone else could ask them for you?" Here are some of their answers:

- Why do parents have more trouble talking to kids than kids have talking to parents?

- Were you a virgin when you got married? Was it worth it?
- Have you ever done something horrible that you regretted?
- Why do you avoid tough issues?
- How would you feel if your child didn't go to college?
- Have either one of you ever had an affair?
- Are you sure, beyond a shadow of a doubt, that this marriage will last any longer than your previous ones?
- Are you willing to admit to your children the mistakes you have made and then ask forgiveness?
- If you had to give up me or your business, which would it be?
- Do you love or even care about me? Do you think I am worthy or can do anything? Why won't you ever listen to me?
- Why is it so important to be a "success"? Is that going to get you to heaven?

Do you know what these kids were saying? They wanted to ask their parents these questions, but they didn't feel the freedom.

Your kids need your example and involvement. And they need to have the freedom to put you on the hot seat. It is better to be embarrassed by a question you don't want to answer than to raise a child who will become a fool and humiliate you later.

Discuss: For only the courageous: Take this list of questions and show them to your teenager. Have him or her mark off which ones he or she would like you to answer someday.

Pray: Thank God for His grace and forgiveness through faith in Jesus Christ.

DAUGHTERS NEED FATHERS, TOO

*Let our . . . daughters [be] as corner pillars
fashioned as for a palace.*

PSALM 144:12

We read a lot today of the problems that occur when boys grow up without male role models. But did you know that a father is also important in helping girls understand their sexual identities?

Boys are not the only ones who lack a sense of how a man should behave. Many young girls don't know either, because they aren't exposed to healthy male-female relationships.

How do you give your daughter a healthy perspective of male-female relationships?

The most influential way is by *how you treat her mother*. As she sees you loving your wife, giving preference to her and giving to her in a sacrificial way, she will learn how a man should treat a woman.

Second, *your daughter needs to know you love her.* She needs to be assured of your protection and your guidance. She will feel a greater sense of self-esteem if she is assured of your love. Hug her. Kiss her. Appropriately express affection for her, even as she matures and goes through adolescence.

Another important way you influence your daughter is *through your spiritual guidance.* She should be shaped by Scripture and by prayer to be "corner pillars fashioned as for a palace"!

Corner—like her role, designed by God to be supportive yet essential to holding a home together.

Pillars—because her inner strength is derived from a confidence and faith in God.

Fashioned—as you guide her to have a soft heart, willing to be led by God's Spirit.

For a palace—because her inner beauty attracts others to Jesus as much as it makes her willing to follow a godly man.

I pray the next generation of women will be pillars of love, faith and commitment to the husbands, families and communities that need them. Maybe with godly fathers involved, millions of little girls will develop into women who will, in turn, build godly families.

Discuss: Evaluate together your involvement as a father in each of your daughters' lives. Prayerfully establish some goals for the upcoming year for each of these relationships.

Pray: Ask God to give you the wisdom to know how to begin influencing your daughters to become "corner pillars fashioned as for a palace."

As she sees you loving
your wife, giving
preference to her and
giving to her in a
sacrificial way, Your
Daughter will learn
how a man should
treat a woman.

"*I* BELIEVE IN YOU!"

Love . . . believes all things.

1 CORINTHIANS 13:4-7

What's the one thing every teenager needs as he or she navigates adolescence? What is needed by every young mother as she assumes a responsibility she's never had before: being a mom? By every athlete to achieve his or her ultimate performance? By every husband to become the man God made him to be?

To be believed in.

All of us need someone to express positive expectancy about our lives.

Two boyhood friends, Johnny and Marty, loved baseball and each other so much that they made a pact to play together always—regardless of what happened. As time went on, Johnny became a baseball star, and his coach called him aside and told him about the upcoming tryouts for the minor leagues. Johnny said, "That's great. Marty and I will sign up right away."

But the coach responded, "Don't worry about Marty. He's just an ugly duckling—too skinny, too slow, can't field and can't hit."

But Johnny's response was "I know he can make it if he has a chance. He's got determination. He can learn to field and hit."

Sure enough, training camp resulted in a contract for Johnny—but Marty was cut. Johnny, however, wouldn't sign without Marty, so the club gave in and awarded a contract to each of them.

Motivated by his friend's actions, Marty slowly began to improve. During their third year in the minor leagues, Johnny washed out and quit. Marty became the rising star. Eventually he was called up to the majors for the St. Louis Cardinals as a shortstop. He played in four World Series and seven All-Star games, and in 1944 he was named Most Valuable Player of the National League.

Years earlier Marty's mom had asked Johnny, "Why are you so determined to keep this pact?"

Johnny replied, "Belief is a kind of love. I believe in Marty. We're friends. Believing in someone is the best kind of love."

Discuss: What communicates affirmative belief to you? In what one area would it most encourage you if someone believed in you more? List an area in which you can show positive belief in your mate and in your children.

Pray: Ask that as a parent you will be able to inspire every member of your household by expressing positive expectations.

LAUGHTER IN THE WALLS

*There is an appointed time for everything. . . . A time to weep,
and a time to laugh; a time to mourn, and a time to dance.*

ECCLESIASTES 3:1-4

The late Bob Benson once wrote that when his kids grew up and left home, he and his wife would sit and listen to the "laughter in the walls."[1] I love that phrase.

Do the walls of your home ring with laughter? Laughter and strong homes go together. A Christian couple should sooner be found guilty of having too much laughter than of having too little. Fun lifts us out of the daily ruts and assassinates the drab, the boring and the mundane. Laughter lightens loads and knits hearts together instantaneously.

God gave children a funny bone and giggle box to balance all of those who are overly intense. He gave our family kids who love to laugh, especially our daughter Rebecca. She lives to laugh. Her beaming smile and giggle is the all-time best. When she would get going at the supper table, pandemonium would break loose. Her giggle box infected us all with uncontrollable, delicious delight. In fact, because of her love for laughter we called her "Rebecca Jean Joy Susie-Q Rainey."

My family taught me how to laugh. Our home was filled with practical jokes, teasing and surprises. I'll never forget my dad's laugh (the best) and my mom's sense of humor. Some of my fondest memories are of laughing so hard that tears just streamed down our faces.

I remember the time my mom gave herself a Hoover vacuum cleaner for Christmas. She wrapped it and put it under the tree with this tag: "To my dear wife, from Ward."

Life is made up of pain, disappointments, pressure, doubts, trials. We are all sapped of strength by these dark, ominous clouds. But, like an exploding shaft of sunlight in a dark room, laughter illuminates life by reminding us not to be so serious.

Why not leave a little laughter in the walls of your home tonight?

Discuss: How was laughter a part of your own home as a child? What laughter have you heard in your present home during the last two days? Is there enough fun in your own heart to spill over and infect other members of your family?

Pray: Ask that the God who calls life from the dead will fill your spirit with new optimism and joy.

Note

1. Source unknown.

THE MOST IMPORTANT THING

For it is He who delivers you from the snare of the trapper.

PSALM 91:3

Some years ago, Barbara and I had the opportunity to enjoy dinner with Dr. James Dobson and his wife, Shirley, of Focus on the Family.

There was one question I had always wanted to ask them, and that night I was able to. "What is the most important thing Barbara and I could do as we raise our kids?"

Without hesitation, both Jim and Shirley looked at us and answered with one word: "Pray." And then they told us why they were so confident about their answer.

One night they had gone to bed when, at about 11:15 P.M., they began to feel uneasy about their daughter, Danae. Jim said he fought the urge to fall asleep. Instead they got out of bed, got down on their knees and prayed for Danae.

Later they learned that, at that very moment, Danae and a friend were in a pull-out curve in the mountains—looking over the lights of the cities below and eating a meal. They were just having a good time when a police car came by and shined a light on them. It made them think to lock their doors. As soon as the police car went by, a bearded man crawled out from under their car and grabbed the door handle, attempting to force his way into the car. They quickly switched on the ignition and sped off. "No one will ever convince me that our prayers did not have an impact in that situation," Jim told us.

That story reminded us how important it is to pray for our children. No matter what you do as parents, in the end it is God who is in control.

Discuss: What are the greatest needs, challenges and pressures of your children right now?

Pray: Ask God to protect your children and deliver them from the snare of evil.

WHEN YOU MAKE
YOUR CHILDREN YOUR
TOP PRIORITY, YOU WILL
RECEIVE MANY BLESSINGS
FROM THE FRUIT
OF YOUR LABOR.

THE PRIVILEGE OF BEING CALLED MOMMY AND DADDY

How blessed is everyone who fears the Lord, who walks in His ways. When you shall eat of the fruit of your hands, you will be happy and it will be well with you.

PSALM 128:1-2

Teddy Roosevelt was unashamedly bullish on children:

> For unflagging interest and enjoyment, a household of children, if things go reasonably well, certainly makes all other forms of success and achievement lose their importance by comparison.[1]

When you make your children your top priority, you will receive many blessings from the fruit of your labor. Barbara and I saw this during a FamilyLife staff banquet in the summer of 1992. We were brought up front for a question-and-answer session, only to be told that the real purpose of the evening was to honor us for our twentieth wedding anniversary.

Several good friends who had been hiding at the back of the room were brought up to say a few words. But the real highlight came when all six of our children showed up to read tributes to us.

Laura, seven at the time, went first, standing on a chair: "Thank you, Mom, for all the dresses you made me. For hugs and kisses. For being a great mom. Dad, thanks for being my ice-cream buddy, for the stories you tell at bedtime and for wrestling with me."

One down, five to go. I looked at Barbara—we both were choking back tears.

Deborah was next. In her quiet, soft voice she thanked her mom for helping her with homework and cutting her hair short. She thanked me for taking her on fishing dates. Then she said, "And I want to thank both of you for adopting me when I was a baby."

That did it! Barbara and I were basket cases for the rest of the evening.

That evening will go down as one of the greatest memories we've ever experienced. Barbara and I count it as our greatest privilege and accomplishment to be called Mommy and Daddy.

Discuss: Prayerfully reflect on the high and holy calling of being a mom and dad. Share why it is such a privilege.

Pray: Ask that you will never forget that children are a blessing.

Note

1. Theodore Roosevelt, *Theodore Roosevelt: An Autobiography* (New York: MacMillan Publishers, Ltd., 1913), n.p.

Since attending a FamilyLife Conference, the Millers have been too distracted to read their favorite books ...

another love story has their attention.

Get away for a romantic weekend together ...

or join us for a life-changing, one-day conference!

FamilyLife has been bringing couples the wonderful news of God's blueprints for marriage since 1976.

Today we are strengthening hundreds of thousands of homes each year in the United States and around the world through:

♦ **Weekend to Remember**™ conferences

♦ **I Still Do**® conferences

♦ **HomeBuilders Couples Series**® small-group Bible studies

♦ **"FamilyLife Today,"** our daily, half-hour radio program, and four other nationally syndicated broadcasts

♦ A comprehensive Web site, **www.familylife.com**, featuring marriage and parenting tips, daily devotions, conference information, and a wide range of resources for strengthening families

♦ Unique marriage and family **connecting resources**

Through these outreaches, FamilyLife is effectively developing godly families who reach the world one home at a time.

FAMILYLIFE™
Bringing Timeless Principles Home

Dennis Rainey, Executive Director
1-800-FL-TODAY (358-6329)
www.familylife.com

A division of Campus Crusade for Christ

Also from Dennis and Barbara Rainey

More Devotions for Drawing Near to God and One Another

Moments Together for Intimacy
Gift Hardcover • ISBN 08307.32489

Moments Together for Parents
Gift Hardcover • ISBN 08307.32497

Moments Together for
Growing Closer to God
Gift Hardcover • ISBN 08307.32500

Moments Together
for a Peaceful Home
Gift Hardcover • ISBN 08307.32519